The Overcoming series was initiated by PETER COOPER, Professor of Psychology at the University of Reading and Honorary NHS Consultant Clinical Psychologist. His original book on bulimia nervosa and binge-eating founded the series in 1993 and continues to help many thousands of people in the USA, the UK and Europe. The aim of the series is to help people with a wide range of common problems and disorders to take control of their own recovery program using the latest techniques of cognitive behavioural therapy. Each book, with its specially tailored program, is devised by a practising clinician. Many books in the Overcoming series are now recommended by the UK Department of Health under the Books on Prescription scheme. Self-help (books and other reading materials based on cognitive behavioural therapy principles) is one of the top three treatments for panic disorder, recommended by the National Institute for Health and Clinical Excellence (NICE).

PROFESSOR DERRICK SILOVE is a clinical psychiatrist and Director of the Centre for Population Mental Health Research and the Psychiatry Research and Teaching Unit at the School of Psychiatry, the University of New South Wales. He has worked for many years in the area of anxiety and traumatic stress, his main area of clinical work, research, service development and teaching. ASSOCIATE PROFESSOR VIJAYA MANICAVASAGAR is a Senior Clinical Psychologist and Associate Professor within the Black Dog Institute, School of Psychiatry at the University of New South Wales. As the Director of Psychological Services at the Black Dog Institute she is responsible for developing and implementing a range of education programs for training mental health professionals in the diagnosis and treatment of mood disorders. Vijaya maintains a strong interest in the anxiety disorders and has published widely in this field.

Other titles in the Overcoming series:

3-part self-help courses

Overcoming Anxiety Self-Help Course
Overcoming Bulimia Nervosa and Binge-Eating Self-Help Course
Overcoming Low Self-Esteem Self-Help Course
Overcoming Social Anxiety and Shyness Self-Help Course

Self-help course single-volume books

Overcoming Anger and Irritability
Overcoming Anorexia Nervosa
Overcoming Anxiety
Bulimia Nervosa and Binge-Eating
Overcoming Childhood Trauma
Overcoming Chronic Fatigue
Overcoming Chronic Pain
Overcoming Compulsive Gambling
Overcoming Depression
Overcoming Insomnia and Sleep Problems
Overcoming Low Self-Esteem
Overcoming Mood Swings
Overcoming Obsessive Compulsive Disorder
Overcoming Panic
Overcoming Paranoid and Suspicious Thoughts
Overcoming Problem Drinking
Overcoming Relationship Problems
Overcoming Sexual Problems
Overcoming Social Anxiety and Shyness
Overcoming Traumatic Stress
Overcoming Weight Problems
Overcoming Your Smoking Habit

All titles in this series are available by mail order.
Please see the order form at the back of this workbook.
www.overcoming.co.uk

OVERCOMING PANIC AND AGORAPHOBIA SELF-HELP COURSE

A 3-part programme based on Cognitive Behavioural Techniques

Part Three: Dealing with Panic Attacks – a self-help manual Steps 4–6

Derrick Silove

and Vijaya Manicavasagar

ROBINSON
London

Constable & Robinson Ltd
3 The Lanchesters
162 Fulham Palace Road
London W6 9ER
www.overcoming.co.uk

First published in the UK by Robinson,
an imprint of Constable & Robinson Ltd 2006

Important Note

This book is not intended as a substitute for medical advice or treatment.
Any person with a condition requiring medical attention should consult
a qualified medical practitioner or suitable therapist.

ISBN-13: 978-1-84529-439-7 (Pack ISBN)
ISBN-10: 1-84529-439-4

ISBN-13: 978-1-84529-549-3 (Part One)
ISBN-10: 1-84529-549-8

ISBN-13: 978-1-84529-550-9 (Part Two)
ISBN-10: 1-84529-550-1

ISBN-13: 978-1-84529-551-6 (Part Three)
ISBN-10: 1-84529-551-X

1 3 5 7 9 10 8 6 4 2

Printed and bound in the EU

Contents

Introduction   vii

SECTION 1: Step 4 – Changing Unhelpful Thinking Styles   1

SECTION 2: Step 5 – Dealing with Physical Sensations   17

SECTION 3: Step 6 – Overcoming Agoraphobia and Troubleshooting Problem Areas   25

SECTION 4: Preventing Setbacks   41

A Final Note   47

Useful Books   48

Useful Addresses   49

Extra Charts and Worksheets   55

Thoughts and Reflections   65

Introduction: How to Use this Workbook

This is a self-help course for dealing with panic and agoraphobia. It has two aims:

1 To help you develop a better understanding of panic and agoraphobia

2 To teach you practical skills to help you manage and overcome your symptoms

Using a self-help approach

A number of techniques are available to control and manage panic attacks. The Overcoming Panic Self-Help Course will guide you through some of these skills to help yourself. The course is divided into three parts and offers a first step in combating panic attacks and agoraphobia. You can work through the course on your own or with a friend, or your may like to work with the support of your healthcare practitioner or therapist.

What does the course involve?

The three workbooks include a number of questionnaires, charts, worksheets and practical exercises for you to work through. Part One helps you to understand anxiety and panic, and Parts Two and Three set out a six-step self-help course to help you systematically overcome these problems. Part One will probably take two to three weeks to complete, while Parts Two and Three may each take three to four weeks to work through.

It is important to take your time and make sure you are happy with each stage before you move on to the next. There is more detailed information about working through the six-step course provided at the beginning of Part Two.

Will I benefit from the course?

There are broadly four groups of people who should find this course helpful:

1 People who have panic attacks, with or without agoraphobia, and are interested in learning specific skills to combat anxiety and control panic symptoms and agoraphobia.

2 People who have had panic attacks in the past and who want to learn techniques to prevent the symptoms coming back. Getting to know the early symptoms and how to combat them will help you feel confident about preventing relapse.

3 People who are familiar with the basic principles of anxiety management but who have not incorporated these skills into a structured programme. The skills are likely to be less effective if you use them in a haphazard manner or if you don't practise them regularly.

4 Relatives and friends who want to support you by getting a better understanding of panic disorder and agoraphobia. It's sometimes difficult for the people close to you to know how to help or what to suggest. Getting their support can be very useful, as long as they offer appropriate and constructive advice and support.

What does each part cover?

Part One explains:

- What panic disorder and agoraphobia are

- How panic disorder and agoraphobia affect people's lives

- What causes panic and agoraphobia

- How panic disorder and agoraphobia can be treated

- The defining features of panic attacks, panic disorder and agoraphobia

Part Two explains:

- How to use the six-step course

- Step 1: how to recognize when you are anxious and identify panic triggers

- Step 2: how to change lifestyle factors that contribute to panic attacks

- Step 3: how to control panic attacks

Part Three explains:

- Step 4: how to challenge unhelpful thinking styles

- Step 5: how to deal with physical sensations

- Step 6: how to overcome agoraphobia and troubleshoot problem areas

- How to prevent setbacks

How to get the most from the course

Here are some tips to help you get the most from the course:

- These workbooks are practical tools – you don't need to keep the pages pristine. Use the space provided to complete the exercises, and feel free to use the pages to jot down any thoughts or notes, or highlight anything that's particularly useful. This will keep all of your notes in one place, which will be helpful when you come to read back through them later on.

- Keep an open mind and be willing to experiment with new ideas and skills. These workbooks will sometimes ask you to think about painful issues. This may be difficult, but if anxiety, panic and agoraphobia are restricting your life it's worth making the effort to overcome these problems – the rewards will be substantial.

- It's important to commit to the course to get the most out of it – so set aside up to half an hour each day to complete the practical exercises.

- Try to answer all of the questions and complete all of the exercises, even if you have to come back to some of them later. There may be times when you get stuck and can't think of how to take things forward. If this happens, don't get angry with yourself or give up. Just put the workbook aside and come back to it later, when you're feeling more relaxed.

- You may find it helpful to have the support of a friend – two heads are often better than one. And if both of you are working through the course you may be able to encourage each other to carry on, even when one of you is finding it hard.

- Use the 'Thoughts and Reflections' section at the back of each workbook to write down anything that you find particularly helpful.

- Reread the workbooks. You may get more out of them once you've had a chance to think about some of the ideas and put them into practice.

- The course is designed so that each workbook builds on what has already been covered – for instance, what you learn in Part One will help you when you come to Part Two. While you can dip into the different sections of Part One, it's important to work through the six-step course in Parts Two and Three systematically. Don't progress to the next step until you've practised and mastered the previous one. It doesn't matter how long it takes you to work through the six steps – what's most important is to understand the techniques and practise the skills.

When should you seek further assistance?

Some people with symptoms of panic may need more help and support than these workbooks can provide. If you fall into one of the seven categories described below, it's likely that you'll benefit from the help of a doctor or therapist:

1 People who have any of the rare physical conditions that mimic panic attacks – described in Section 3 of Part One. It's important to consult your doctor if you suspect that you may have one of these conditions.

2 People with severe agoraphobia – especially if it is unrelated to symptoms of panic. These workbooks are for people suffering primarily from panic disorder, who may or may not have some degree of agoraphobia.

3 People with severe depression associated with panic disorder, who might not have the motivation to work through a self-help book on their own. There's a brief guide to managing depression after this introduction.

4 People who lack the confidence to work on their own, or who feel that a self-help course isn't enough. It's important to be fully motivated to follow this course – if you practise the techniques half-heartedly you're unlikely to get good results.

5 People with a strong resistance to making changes in their life.

6 People who have panic attacks and agoraphobia as only one aspect of wider emotional, social or personality problems. For example, if you respond to stress by misusing drugs or alcohol, you may need to seek counselling for substance abuse before (or at the same time as) trying to overcome panic disorder.

7 People with severe mental health issues – for example people who are severely depressed or have psychosis. In these cases it's important to seek the help of a mental health professional.

A Note on Depression

It's quite common for depression and anxiety to go hand in hand. But if you have panic disorder it's unlikely that you'll feel depressed all of the time – it's more usual for these feelings to be fleeting or relatively minor. It might be that you feel depressed for a short while because you've experienced a setback or that you're having to cope with more everyday stress than you've been used to for a while. Some people experience a few days of depressed mood following a panic attack.

As long as you feel positive about life most of the time, it's likely that you'll be able to sustain your energy and motivation to continue learning and practising the techniques to help you overcome panic attacks and agoraphobia. But if you find that you're depressed all or most of the time, and this feeling becomes overwhelming, it's time to get some professional help.

How to deal with minor depression

You can use a self-help approach to combat minor bouts of depression that last a few hours or days. Try these steps:

- Write a list of the stressors that are making you feel depressed, and use the problem-solving technique you learnt in Step 6 to work through any problems.

- Use the techniques in Step 3 to focus your mind on things that you enjoy or which give you pleasure. This is a good approach if you can't easily deal with whatever's making you feel depressed.

- Negative thinking can make you feel depressed. So take another look at Step 4, where you learnt how to identify and challenge negative thinking, and substitute these unhelpful thoughts with more positive and constructive ones.

Dealing with depression

Write down the stressors you face and try to work out step-by-step strategies to deal with them

Do something that helps raise your self-esteem – engage in an activity that's pleasurable and non-stressful

Examine whether your thoughts about yourself, your situation and the future are excessively negative. Challenge these negative thoughts and try to replace them with helpful ones

If your symptoms persist, or if you feel desperate and you're unable to cope, seek professional help

Regular counselling sessions   Hospitalization
and/or medication

It's important to get some professional help if these self-help techniques don't make you feel better, or you start to feel hopeless or desperate. Don't try to battle it out yourself – there's lots of support available if you ask for help.

Your doctor may suggest an antidepressant medicine and/or regular counselling sessions to help you get through your depression. If you're severely depressed, you may need intensive treatment such as a stay in hospital – being looked after like this can help your recovery and protect you from neglecting or harming yourself and eventually put you back on the road to recovery.

SECTION 1: Step 4 – Changing Unhelpful Thinking Styles

This section will help you understand:

- How to identify negative thinking styles

- How to challenge your negative thoughts

- How to change your negative thoughts to more positive ones

There have probably been times in your life when you've been extremely worried – about your health, your family or friends, your job, your finances or your future. It's normal to worry about things and it's a useful way to anticipate problems and work out ways to solve them or find a way forward. But if you worry too much it can become a problem in itself – for instance if you're constantly worried about being made redundant it can stop you focusing on the good things about your job, or what's going well at home.

   If you're constantly worrying about these things, and the worry becomes intense, you're likely to start feeling the physical effects. You might:

- Have tense muscles – if your neck muscles are tense you may have headaches

- Sweat more than usual

- Feel your stomach churning

- Have a dry feeling in your throat and mouth

Some people find that this increasing tension can trigger panic attacks. And as you discovered in the earlier sections, a number of other things can also make you feel more anxious and stressed:

- The physical symptoms of anxiety, such as a pounding heart, can make you worry about your health. For instance you may think you've got some sort of serious illness, which can make you feel even more anxious.

- Being tired and run down, and not eating properly or getting enough exercise can make your symptoms of stress and anxiety worse.

- Not getting enough sleep, a poor diet and other physical factors can reduce your resistance to stress (the mind-body link).

- Hyperventilation or overbreathing can trigger panic attacks.

Step 4 shows you how to deal with worrying thoughts or negative thinking styles, which can make you more vulnerable to anxiety and panic attacks. You can do this by using this three-stage process:

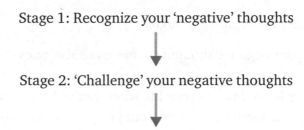

Stage 1: Recognize your 'negative' thoughts

Stage 2: 'Challenge' your negative thoughts

Stage 3: Substitute these thoughts with 'positive' or more helpful thoughts

How to identify negative thinking

The way in which you interpret experiences, situations and sensations influences the way you feel about them, and your emotional reactions to these things. For example, if you think that you're going to have a panic attack in a shopping centre, you may find that you become very nervous every time you go shopping. This is called anticipatory anxiety (see Part One, Section 1). So just by predicting that you'll become anxious in a particular situation, you increase the chances of actually having a panic attack. It's a vicious circle again:

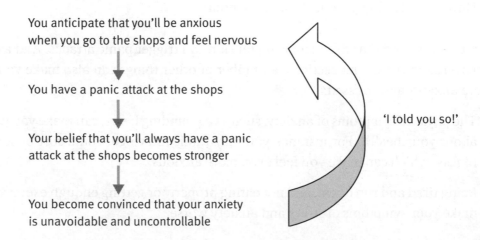

You anticipate that you'll be anxious when you go to the shops and feel nervous

You have a panic attack at the shops

Your belief that you'll always have a panic attack at the shops becomes stronger

You become convinced that your anxiety is unavoidable and uncontrollable

'I told you so!'

When you eventually have a panic attack, it strengthens your belief that you will always have a panic attack in that situation – in effect, you're giving yourself a negative message: 'I told you so!'

This is how your ideas, thoughts and beliefs can lead to unpleasant emotions like anxiety, anger or depression. And because these emotions are so unpleasant, you may start to avoid situations where you predict that these feelings are likely to occur. So it's not the *actual* places or events that upset you – it's your *interpretations* and *expectations* of these places or events that cause the problem.

Most situations can be interpreted in different ways. But you may be in the habit of interpreting things in a way that regularly creates feelings of anxiety and panic. You can change this though, and reduce your anxious reactions by practising alternative – but realistic – interpretations of these situations.

Here are some examples of negative thoughts:

- 'I know for sure that I'll have a panic attack if I go into any department store'

- 'I'm definitely going to faint and no one will help me'

- 'This pain in my chest must be a heart attack. I'm going to die'

- 'Everyone will laugh at me if I have a panic attack here'

- 'Once panic starts, nothing can stop it'

You may have unhelpful thoughts such as these again and again in certain situations. And these 'automatic' thoughts can suddenly appear in your mind without you even being fully aware of them. It's as if you've got a 'hidden commentator' in your mind, predicting doom and gloom. This tendency to interpret situations negatively can be influenced by many things, such as your upbringing, the expectations of your family and friends, and by some of your experiences.

One of the most unhelpful aspects of these interpretations is that they are over-generalizations. For example, if you have a panic attack on a bus, you may then believe that travelling on trains, planes, or any form of transport will also bring on an attack. These ideas cause a vicious cycle. And because you then tend to avoid the situations that you predict will make you frightened and anxious, you avoid testing out these over-generalizations, so you're never able to find out how unhelpful or untrue they really are. So if you've stopped going to department stores for instance, you won't know if you'd still have a panic attack if you walked into one today. This vicious cycle effectively locks you into a restricted life of fear.

The table below shows two examples of negative thoughts and the situations in which they occur. Fill in the blank spaces below these examples with any negative thoughts you've had in difficult situations.

Situation	Negative thought
Shopping in a department store	'I can't cope with this anxiety'
Appointment at the hairdresser	'What if I have a panic attack and can't get out quickly?'

Some examples of negative thinking styles

You can group these negative or faulty thinking styles into several types, but all of them simply increase your anxiety levels or make you feel despondent or demoralized. Albert Ellis, a therapist specializing in methods of challenging negative attitudes, highlighted the seven examples of faulty thinking styles listed below. See if you recognize some of these thinking styles:

1 **Black-and-white thinking** or seeing an event as either a total success or a total failure, with no room for anything in-between. For example, you might say to yourself: 'If I experience any anxiety symptoms when I go shopping, then I've failed completely in managing my anxiety.'

2 **Generalizing** from one situation to the next. If one situation doesn't work out well, then you may decide that all similar situations will also be difficult. For example: 'I was feeling panicky at the train station so I know I'll be panicky whenever I try to take public transport', or 'I'm still experiencing some panicky symptoms when I go out, so I know I can't go anywhere any more.' This 'over-generalizing' can set up a vicious cycle of avoidance.

3 **Magnifying unpleasant experiences or focusing only on negatives.** For example: 'I chaired a meeting and caught up with all my paperwork, but I then became panicky when I couldn't find an important folder. The whole day was a complete write-off.'

4 **Overestimating failure and underestimating success.** For example: 'So what if I am a successful journalist? I'm a worthless person because I suffer from anxiety symptoms', or 'Everyone thinks that I'm a total failure because I have panic attacks.'

5 **Setting unrealistic expectations** and not allowing yourself to make any mistakes. For example: 'I am practising all my anxiety management skills so I expect to never suffer from a panic attack again', or 'I expect to be cured by next week.'

6 **Taking responsibility for others' feelings.** For example: 'It's my fault that the party was a failure – it must be because I was anxious', or 'It's my fault that my anxiety symptoms make my family upset.'

7 **Mind-reading other people's thoughts** or assuming certain outcomes without checking the facts. For example: 'They think I'm stupid because I suffer from panic attacks', or 'I know for sure that I will have a panic attack if I try to drive over the bridge.'

If you think about it, you might find that you're using some of these negative thinking styles without even being aware that you're doing this. And remember that these thoughts can become habitual, flashing through your mind, and upsetting you without you even realizing exactly why.

Try this four-step exercise every time you become even slightly upset or anxious:

1 Say 'STOP' to yourself

2 Then try to work out exactly what train of thought led to that feeling

3 See if you can link the negative thoughts to anything that has happened or been said recently

4 Think about it – can you detect a particular pattern in your negative thinking?

Challenging your negative thoughts

Once you've identified your negative thinking habits, the next step is to learn how to change those thoughts to more positive, appropriate ones. This involves critically examining your thoughts and considering how accurate they really are. Here are three ways of challenging your negative thoughts.

- **Questioning the evidence for the negative thought** You may need to examine the chances of a negative thought being true all of the time. For example, to challenge the thought 'I am sure to have a panic attack if I go into the department store', think whether you automatically have panic attacks in all department stores. What evidence do you have that suggests you will definitely have a panic attack in this situation? Try to recall the times when you did not have an attack, or had only minor symptoms of anxiety when you were shopping. Another way of questioning the evidence for a negative thought is to check whether you have unrealistic expectations of yourself. Are you expecting yourself to never experience any symptoms of anxiety when you go shopping? Is this realistic?

- **Checking out other possibilities before you jump to a conclusion** Before you decide that your negative interpretation of yourself or of a situation is the only 'correct' one, think about alternative ways of interpreting the same situation. For example, if you experience sensations such as not feeling 'with it', or being slightly dizzy, weak or feeling hot, try to think about other possible causes: did you stand up too quickly after sitting for a long time? Were you feeling excited? Was the room too hot? Were there other things that could have produced some of those sensations? Was the weather hot or were you tired? Did you have a viral illness, or were you doing strenuous exercise?

- **Asking others for their interpretation of a situation** This can be a useful method, especially if you're with someone who can give you an accurate account of a particular event. Close friends, work colleagues, relatives or your spouse or partner can often help you to see a situation from a different, and possibly more realistic, perspective.

Try challenging some of your own negative thoughts by completing the exercise below:

1 Look at the two examples in the table on the next page

2 Now choose three recent instances when you felt anxious and identify the situations you were in

3 Think about the negative thoughts you experienced on each occasion

4 Try challenging those thoughts using the strategies of 'questioning the evidence' and 'checking out other possibilities'

5 Do you notice that your anxiety level changes when you start to challenge your negative thoughts?

There are blank tables at the back of this workbook if you need them.

Challenging negative thoughts

Situation	Negative thought	Challenging thought and considering an alternative
Going to the supermarket on a hot day and experiencing panic symptoms	'I'll never get better'	'It was hot and I was rushing. Next time I'll take it slower, choose a less busy time and make sure to stop for a drink. I have already made some progress and if I continue to improve, I will eventually get better'
Visiting family and having a heated discussion; feeling dizzy and having a pounding heart	'I'm going to have a heart attack'	'I have been through several medical investigations and there is nothing wrong with my heart. My symptoms improved as soon as we left. I must have become overexcited. I know that if I was having a heart attack, I would not be feeling better so quickly'

Changing your negative thoughts to positive ones

In the last two sections you looked at how negative thoughts about yourself and your ability to cope in different situations can lead to anxiety symptoms and panic attacks. You also saw that by challenging these thoughts, you can feel less anxious by making your excessive worries less 'believable'. The next stage in overcoming your negative thoughts is to substitute more positive and helpful thoughts for the unpleasant, unhelpful ones.

So rather than thinking those gloomy or fearful thoughts that can make you anxious, what would you like to be able to say to yourself instead? Most people would like to be able to say 'I can cope with this' or 'I'll be all right'. What sorts of encouraging thoughts would you like to say to yourself the next time you come across a difficult situation? Look at the examples below and then add some of the things you would like to think in the situations that worry you.

Examples of positive thinking

Situation	Helpful thought
Department store	'I can handle my anxiety'
Hairdresser	'I am going to enjoy having my hair cut'

Now try the process for yourself:

1   Think back to the last time you felt anxious or panicky and try to recall the kinds of negative thoughts that were going through your mind. First describe the situation:

Situation:

_____

_____

_____

_____

_____

2   Now write down any negative thoughts that you remember, either about yourself or about the situation.

Negative thoughts:

_____

_____

_____

_____

_____

_____

3   What can you say to yourself to challenge those negative thoughts? Try questioning the evidence for them, using the techniques in the previous sections of Step 4. What could you say to yourself to make the negative thoughts less 'believable'?

Challenging thoughts:

_____

_____

_____

_____

_____

_____

4 Now that you've challenged those negative thoughts, do you notice that you're not as anxious about the situation? Have you managed to make your negative thoughts less 'believable'? If you have, then the final stage is to substitute more positive, helpful thoughts about the same situation. What encouraging things could you say to yourself?

Helpful thoughts:

_____

_____

_____

_____

_____

_____

_____

At first, this exercise may seem a bit difficult. But with practice you'll find that it becomes easier to recognize and challenge your negative thoughts and, finally, to substitute more helpful, positive thoughts about yourself and the things you do. Use the monitoring form on the next page to help you practise this technique. There are extra forms at the end of the book if you need them.

Rate your anxiety level from '0' to '10', where:

- '0' is 'not at all anxious'

- '10' is 'extremely anxious'

Self-monitoring form for changing negative thoughts

Day/date	Negative thought	Anxiety level	Challenging thought	Positive/helpful thought

More ways to help change your negative thoughts

1 How many times have you thought to yourself that you can give other people good advice about coping with stress but you can't solve similar problems of your own? So why not try giving yourself some of your own good advice, as if you were advising a good friend whose problems you understand very well? Think for a minute, and write down what you'd say to someone who has asked for your advice about anxiety and panic attacks?

_____

_____

_____

_____

2 Another technique is to imagine someone you know who always manages to look on the bright side of a difficult situation. Sometimes, just putting yourself in someone else's shoes can help you to look at a situation differently, especially if that person has a positive outlook on life. How would this person interpret a situation that you find difficult? See if you can write down some of the positive, encouraging thoughts that this person would think.

_____

_____

_____

_____

3 You can also check your own thoughts about a situation with someone who is close to you and knows you fairly well. Try to develop a habit of discussing the way you see a situation with someone else – find out whether that situation makes them feel tense or anxious. Someone else might immediately see the negative aspect of your way of thinking when it's not obvious to you. This could help you practise 'thinking straight' by looking at alternative explanations for situations you find difficult. Try not to hold onto particular negative interpretations of yourself and of the situations you encounter. Instead, get into the habit of looking at a situation from different perspectives.

4 'Cue cards' can be a useful way to remind yourself to think more helpful, encouraging thoughts. These are small cards that you can carry in your purse or wallet and read whenever you feel yourself slipping back into negative thinking styles. Write a single helpful thought on each card and use as many cards as you like. Read through the cards whenever you need to remind yourself to think positively. You can use them when you're out shopping, while you're on the bus, or in any other situation that you might find difficult. With practice, these helpful thoughts will become 'second nature' to you and, in time, you may not even need to use the cards any more.

Summary

Review of Step 4

By now you'll be better at recognizing your negative thoughts, and challenging and changing them to more positive, helpful thoughts. Remember that it has taken time to develop your usual thinking styles so, like any other habit, they take time and practice to change. It's important to reward yourself for over-coming each negative thought – this can be a helpful way to break the habit of thinking negatively. Try to reward yourself whenever you 'think straight' and manage to overcome your anxiety.

Review your progress by answering the following questions (circle 'yes' or 'no' where relevant):

1 Can you identify some of your negative thoughts that may be leading to anxiety and panic?

  Yes   No

2 Are you effectively challenging your negative thoughts?

  Yes   No

3 What positive or helpful thoughts would you like to substitute for those negative thoughts?

4 Have you developed a list of cue cards to use when you feel anxious?

  Yes   No

5 Are you using your cards regularly?

  Yes   No

If you're able to answer 'yes' to questions 1, 2, 4 and 5, go on to Step 5, which deals with your anxieties about the physical sensations of panic.

SECTION 2: Step 5 – Dealing with Physical Sensations

This section will help you understand:

- How to overcome fear of 'normal' physical sensations

- How to challenge your catastrophic thoughts about physical sensations

If you have panic disorder, normal physical sensations such as being sweaty or having a pounding heart – how you might feel if you ran for the bus on a hot day – may remind you of symptoms of panic. And these feelings can make you feel worried and anxious. If you're very worried about your health over a long period of time, these concerns can trigger panic attacks. This is another vicious cycle – physical symptoms trigger panic attacks, and feeling panicky turns your focus onto these physical sensations.

Have you noticed that certain changes in the way your body feels – such as your heart beating faster when you're walking – make you worry that you could be having a panic attack? If you do, you're not alone – many people with panic disorder feel like this. You've started to fear 'normal' physical sensations, because you're mistaking them for signs of imminent panic.

Think about which physical sensations remind you of symptoms of panic. Use the space below to write a list of the ones you associate with feelings of anxiety and panic:

1 _____

2 _____

3 _____

4 _____

5 _____

Have you started to avoid certain activities because they're more likely to trigger worrying physical symptoms? Many people with panic disorder avoid strenuous activity and regular exercise for just this reason. For example, going for a swim might make you feel out of breath. But if you don't do any exercise, you'll become physically unfit and this can make you more vulnerable to stress.

You might also find that you're the type of person who will go to any length to avoid having confrontations with people. The emotions that come from having arguments and disagreements can make your face flush and your mouth and throat feel dry, as well as making your breathing more shallow. These sensations are very similar to the feelings you get during a panic attack. So to avoid these sensations, you might find it easier to simply 'give in' to your friends and family, or agree with them too easily, just to keep the peace. But being unassertive can become a habit and this leads to other problems, such as not standing up for yourself when you really should.

If you're going to break this chain of negative events, it's important to recognize the activities or situations that you're avoiding because you don't want to feel the physical sensations you associate with panic. Use the space below to make a list of some of the situations that you avoid – along with the physical sensations that they produce:

	Activity	*Physical sensations*
1		
2		
3		
4		
5		

Learning to overcome fear of 'normal' physical sensations

Step 5 will cover two of the methods you can use to help you overcome your fears of the 'normal' physical sensations that remind you of panic attacks. Try practising both of them to see which works best for you – in time you should be able to accept these feelings in your body without becoming anxious.

Desensitization or exposure

The trick to this first technique is to let yourself experience the normal physical sensations of anxiety – such as feeling your heart beat faster – while using the techniques you've already learnt to control your anxiety levels. You'll soon find that it's difficult to remain anxious when you experience the same sensation over and over again without suffering any negative effects. In Step 3 you learnt a breathing technique to help you control your anxiety and panic attacks. You can use this technique to help you overcome your fears of physical sensations.

Go back to your list of feared physical sensations. Can you think of something you could do to produce these sensations? The list below suggests some things you could do to bring on the sensations that remind you of panic symptoms:

Physical sensation	How to produce this sensation
Rapid heart rate	Physical activity such as walking, slow jogging, walking up and down stairs or doing push-ups or sit-ups.
Sweating	Physical activity (see above) or walking about in hot weather, taking a hot bath or wearing warm clothes.
Trembling or muscle weakness	Make a fist and squeeze hard: hold the tension in your hand for a few minutes and then suddenly release it.
Shortness of breath, panting	Exercises such as fast walking, slow jogging or swimming.
Dizziness	Spin around slowly with your eyes open, or spin slowly on a swivel chair.

Doing vigorous exercise naturally makes you breathe faster, so the slow breathing technique you learnt in Step 3 isn't any good for controlling the breathlessness you'll feel when you're very active. But the slow breathing technique works well for any of the sensations that aren't produced by vigorous exercise, such as controlling the anxiety you feel when you experience sensations of sweating, dizziness or muscle weakness.

When you're doing something that makes your heart beat faster or makes you short of breath, it's best to 'wait out' these sensations or use the technique described in the next section to control your anxiety. You can also try the muscle relaxation exercise described in Step 2 to reduce your overall level of arousal while you wait out these sensations.

Try using a gradual step-by-step approach that you can include in your exercise programme. Here's an example:

- Choose a walk through a park where you know that there are benches at regular intervals

- Each day, gradually increase the speed at which you walk until the pace makes you sweat and increases your heart rate, and makes you slightly breathless

- Sit down on a bench and practise your mini-muscle relaxation exercise

- Note that the physical sensations gradually fade as you relax and rest

Challenging your catastrophic thoughts about physical sensations

In Step 4 you learnt how to identify, challenge and change the negative thoughts that pop into your head when you're anxious or if you find yourself in a situation that makes you feel anxious. Now you need to apply the same principles to deal with your fears of physical sensations.

What thoughts do you experience when you feel these physical sensations? The table below gives a couple of examples – use the space beneath these examples to write down some of your own thoughts.

Examples of catastrophic thinking about physical sensations	
Physical sensation	Fearful thought
1 Rapid heart rate	'I'm having a heart attack'
2 Light-headedness	'I'm going crazy' or 'I'm going to faint'
3	
4	
5	
6	

In Step 4 you learnt how to challenge these negative thoughts by questioning the evidence, checking out other possibilities before you jump to conclusions, and asking other people about their interpretations of the same situation. You can now use these techniques to challenge your fears of physical sensations. Answer these two questions in the space below:

- What could you say to yourself to make these fears less believable?

_____

_____

_____

_____

- What would be a more sensible way of interpreting your physical sensations?

_____

_____

_____

_____

The last stage of changing your unhelpful thinking styles is to substitute more rational, encouraging thoughts. Try substituting positive, helpful thoughts in the situations where, before, you tended to think negatively about physical sensations. Use the table on the next page to challenge and change your negative thoughts to more helpful ones – there are some examples to guide you. Use the blank tables at the back of this workbook to continue practising this exercise.

Challenging and changing negative thoughts about physical sensations

Physical sensation	Negative thought	Challenging thought	Helpful thought
Sweating	'I'm going to have a panic attack'	'It's a hot day, I must be hot. I'm only sweating because of the heat. I'll just remove my jacket'	'This isn't a panic attack. My sweatiness will go away as I cool down. I can cope'

Summary

Review of Step 5

In Step 5 you've looked at how you can use two techniques to combat your fear of the normal physical sensations, and how to overcome further anxiety you may associate with these sensations.

Review your progress by asking yourself the following questions (circle 'yes' or 'no' where relevant):

1 Have you made a list of the physical sensations that mimic panic?
Yes   No

2 Have you chosen the best methods to produce these sensations?
Yes   No

3 What are your negative thoughts associated with those sensations?

4 Can you challenge those negative thoughts?
Yes   No

5 Have you developed a list of positive, helpful thoughts to substitute for those negative thoughts?
Yes   No

6 Can you think of other anxiety-management techniques you could use to control the anxiety caused by mislabelling physical sensations?
Yes   No

7 Have you written out cue cards to use when you start to react to your physical sensations?
Yes   No

8 Are you using your cards regularly?
Yes   No

If you can answer 'yes' to all the questions (except 3), you're ready to start putting all the skills into practice. When you feel confident about using these skills, you're ready to move on to Step 6, which deals with overcoming anxiety and agoraphobia in difficult situations.

SECTION 3: Step 6 – Overcoming Agoraphobia and Troubleshooting Problem Areas

This section will help you understand:

- What graded exposure is

- How to apply anxiety-management techniques

- How to troubleshoot problem areas

By now you'll be familiar with a number of techniques to control your anxiety symptoms. By practising them regularly, and putting them into practice whenever you start to feel anxious, you'll be able to return gradually to doing the activities that you've been avoiding. So rather than saying no to things you previously enjoyed doing, which may have made life difficult and left you feeling depressed, you'll be able to lead a full life again. For example, if you feared driving you may have been avoiding visiting friends, going shopping or looking for a job. This one fear can lead to major life problems like losing touch with your friends, relying on other people for transport, or experiencing financial hardship.

Although avoiding or withdrawing from stressful situations can reduce your anxiety in the short term, it always leads to other problems that have a big impact on your lifestyle. By working through this six-step course, you'll have learnt that there are other ways of coping with anxiety – ways that don't place unhelpful restrictions on the way you live.

Using graded exposure to overcome your fears

We introduced the idea of graded exposure or systematic desensitization in Part One, Section 4. This is an effective technique for overcoming your fears or phobias of situations that aren't actually dangerous. By repeatedly exposing yourself to the situation that previously frightened you, you uncouple the 'fight or flight' response from the situation.

When you start to practise the graded-exposure technique, you need to keep in mind these six principles:

1 It's important to work out and write down a list of the places and situations that frighten you, and rank them according to the level of anxiety that they provoke – so that top of the list is whatever frightens you most of all.

2 It's best to work through this list systematically, from the bottom up – so start with the situation you fear the least. You may need to break down each task into a series of smaller ones, so that you overcome your fear step-by-step. Don't worry if you need to repeat the first step several times before you get to the point where your anxiety level falls enough to let you attempt the next step. It's also best to try and remain at one step – the situation that scares you – for long enough to let your anxiety fall to a comfortable level before you move up to the next step.

3 Don't try to rush up your list of feared situations. It's important to move forward at a rate that's right for you. You shouldn't ever feel more than moderately anxious – let your anxiety guide the level that you are able to manage. It's better to progress slowly and steadily than to try to take bigger steps than you can manage, only to feel discouraged by a setback.

4 You can use a number of strategies to make the exposure process easier in the early stages of this part of the course. Choose the most useful techniques from the anxiety-management strategies you've practised. You'll find that not all of them will be useful in every situation, so try to plan ahead and think about which ones are likely to be the most useful for each situation. You could make notes on your cue cards to remind you.

5 You might find it helpful to ask someone you trust to help you with the early stages of the exposure exercises. But it's important to explain the purpose of the exercise to your friend and make sure that they understand the process. For instance, they need to agree to withdraw gradually during the course to allow you to develop the confidence to approach the situations that once frightened you, on your own. For the process to work it's critical that both of you accept this and that you're open about it. Your friend may expect quicker progress than you can manage, or you may be tempted to 'hold on' for too long to the security they provide.

6 The most important thing to remember is that you're trying to work systematically – so this means you need to be committed to the course and make it a priority in your life. The best approach is to tackle the tasks one step at a time, practise the exercises regularly, and be willing to take a step back if you have a setback. If you practise the exercises haphazardly, or you give up for days because you've had a 'bad' outing, then the whole process will take much longer. It's a good idea to use a monitoring form (see below) to plot your progress week by week and keep track of your improvement. Doing this will also help you see that even if you have a small setback, it doesn't necessarily mean that you're not making good progress.

How to make your ranked list of stressful situations

Drawing up a list of the situations that make you feel anxious is the first step in overcoming your fear of them. And as you found in Step 1, putting it down on paper also helps you to see what kinds of situations make you feel anxious and helps you to focus on when and how to use the anxiety-management skills you've been practising. These are some examples of the situations that make some people feel anxious:

- Being alone at home

- Walking down the road

- Visiting the supermarket

- Driving over a bridge in heavy traffic

Drawing up your list:

- List the situations that you find stressful in the table on the next page.

- For each situation, rate how anxious you feel on a scale of '0' to '10', where:

  – '0' is 'no anxiety'

  – '10' is your 'highest level of anxiety'

- Remember, it's best to start practising your stress-management skills on the situations you find easier or less stressful.

- Record your rating each week to track whether you're reducing your 'anxiety ratings' for the various situations. Use the spare forms at the back of the book to record extra weeks.

Monitoring anxiety-provoking situations

Situation	Rating (0–10) 0 = no anxiety, 10 = highest level of anxiety	Change in rating		
		Week 1	Week 2	Week 3

Catching a bus – an example of graded exposure

Stepping onto a bus can feel like climbing a mountain if you have agoraphobia. Even if you were once able to catch a bus without feeling anxious, this may have become a situation that you now try to avoid. Here's how you can start to deal with this problem by using graded exposure.

1 Try breaking down the task into three smaller stages:

- Stage 1 – walking to the bus stop

- Stage 2 – catching the bus for one stop

- Stage 3 – catching the bus over the bridge to the shopping centre

2 Plan to tackle stage 1 over three or four days, with the help of a friend. On the first day walk to the bus stop with your friend, sit together in the bus shelter and wait there until you feel less anxious. You may find it useful to practise the mini relaxation exercise you learnt in Step 2 while you're sitting there. Then return home together.

3 Repeat this exercise the next day, and notice whether you feel less anxious.

4 The following day, ask your friend to walk 50 paces behind you and then join you at the bus stop. Within a few days, you'll probably find that you can walk to the bus stop and back on your own – and each time you do this you'll feel less and less anxious.

You're now ready to repeat the process for catching the bus and travelling one stop:

- Begin by asking your friend to get on the bus with you and sit next to you.

- The next day, ask your friend to sit a few seats behind you.

- The following day, ask your friend to see you off at the bus stop and meet you at the next stop.

Gradually, you can progress to catching the bus on your own and staying on it until you reach the shops. And you can adapt this sequence to driving a car, catching a train, walking to a shopping centre or going out to a restaurant. But remember that learning to cope with anxiety is a gradual process that takes practice:

- Start by practising your anxiety-controlling techniques in less distressing situations.

- Once you become more confident, you can apply these skills to more difficult situations.

How to use anxiety-management techniques

You can now start to look at how to combine your stress-management skills to work through some of the more complex situations that make you feel anxious. Remember that you'll need to find the particular combination of techniques and steps that works best for you, and that it's important to work at your own pace. It's a good idea to try a combination of techniques that works on your body as well as your mind:

- In Step 2 you saw that it's important to look after your physical wellbeing by keeping active, eating a good diet and getting enough sleep. You can also use muscle-relaxation exercises to reduce any tension in your body.

- Step 3 covered various ways to help you control panic attacks, such as slow breathing and distraction techniques.

- In Step 4 you looked at how to change negative thinking styles that can knock your confidence and lead to symptoms of anxiety.

In the next two sections you'll learn how to apply the skills you've been practising to two situations that many people with panic disorder find stressful: going to the supermarket and visiting the dentist.

Scenario 1: Going to the supermarket

For this exercise, imagine that you've included 'going to the supermarket' on your list of stressful situations.

1 You can start to prepare before you even leave the house, so begin the day by doing a brief muscle relaxation exercise.

2 You'll need to challenge any negative thoughts that pop into your head when you think about going into the supermarket. You might find it easier to spend a few minutes writing them down before you leave home. You can then challenge them, and substitute them with more helpful, encouraging thoughts that will reduce your anxiety about going to the supermarket. Here's an example:

Negative thoughts	Challenge the negative thought	Helpful thoughts
'I will have a terrible panic attack and lose control.'	'I don't always have panic attacks in supermarkets, and even if I did get panicky, I know how to control my symptoms.' 'I've never lost control or started screaming when I've been to the supermarket, and it is unlikely that I'll do so now.'	'I can cope with this.' 'I know how to keep my anxiety under control.'
'I will look so anxious that other people will think I am crazy.'	'I look anxious, but it's unlikely that people will take special notice of me. Even if they do notice me looking anxious, they will not automatically think I'm crazy. Lots of people look stressed in the supermarket.'	'It will be over soon.'

3 When you get to the supermarket car park, use the slow breathing technique to help you stay calm and relaxed.

4 Use your 'cue' cards to remind yourself of how to challenge your negative thoughts – you can look at them just before you go into the supermarket.

5 Once you're inside, keep your breathing slow and even. Try pacing yourself so that you don't rush through the supermarket feeling overwhelmed and frantic. If you do get anxious, simply stop and focus on slowing your breathing, and read your 'cue' cards to help you challenge any negative thoughts.

6 Try using distraction techniques like counting or visualization while you're waiting at the checkout – you could try counting the items in your basket.

7 Finally, when you've finished shopping, give yourself a small treat as a reward for coping with the situation.

Scenario 2: Visiting the dentist

Lots of people feel anxious and frightened about going to the dentist for a check-up – this may well be on your list of situations that make you feel anxious.

1 You could start preparing for your check-up by making sure you have a good night's sleep.

2 Before you leave home, practise your muscle relaxation exercise.

3 Plan how long it will take to get to the surgery and how you're going to get there. Leave yourself plenty of time so that you don't feel rushed or flustered.

4 Examine your negative thoughts – write them down, challenge them, and think of some helpful thoughts to replace the negative ones. Your list may look something like this:

Negative thoughts	Challenge the negative thought	Helpful thoughts
'I will scream or lose control when the dentist examines me.'	*'I have never screamed or lost control when I have gone to the dentist in the past and it is unlikely that I will do so now.'*	*'Even though it is uncomfortable visiting the dentist, it only lasts for half an hour. I can manage that.'*
'I will be so anxious that I may faint and the dentist will think I'm crazy.'	*'I have never fainted at the dentist's surgery and it is unlikely that I will faint now. If I do feel faint, I can tell the dentist and she will give me time to recover.'*	*'I have ways of controlling my anxiety symptoms.'*
	'The dentist sees many patients who are anxious and it is unlikely that she thinks they are all crazy.'	*'I can cope with going to the dentist. I am prepared for this visit.'*

5 In the dentist's waiting room mentally scan through your body to detect any muscle tension – ask yourself whether your body feels rigid or stiff. You might be clenching your teeth without even realizing it! Carry out a quick muscle-relaxation exercise by focusing on any areas that feel especially tense. As you breathe out, say the word 'RELAX' to yourself. Do this a few times until you begin to feel those muscles actually relaxing and the tension reducing. Focus on your breathing, remembering to keep your breathing rhythm slow and even. If you feel anxious, use your breathing-control technique until you start to feel yourself relax. Try to maintain this feeling of calmness for as long as possible – but simply go back through these exercises if you start to feel your anxiety rising again.

6 Tell your dentist that you feel anxious and that you may need a little time between procedures to regain your equilibrium. You can also ask the dentist to explain each procedure to you and say how long it will take. It's worth chatting through what's going to happen – most dentists will agree beforehand to stop a procedure if you lift your hand up to signal that you need a break.

7 Reward yourself with a small treat for coping with your anxiety when the visit is over.

Troubleshooting problem areas

Some of the problems you face in life can be complex or deep-rooted – they may have arisen from something you experienced as a child for instance. It's beyond the scope of this self-help book to deal with these problems – it's better to think about seeing a counsellor if there are specific issues you want to work through. But there are techniques you can learn to help you deal with everyday problems.

Over the years, you've probably developed your own way of dealing with these day-to-day problems – and if you were to talk to a friend you might find that they tackle their problems in a different way entirely. There's no 'best' way of solving problems, but some ways are better than others – especially in the long run.

One way of 'dealing' with problems is to simply ignore them. But if you don't tackle these issues as they arise, you can begin to feel helpless and frustrated as they mount up at the back of your mind. This can eventually make your panic symptoms worse. Here are some common but ineffective ways of coping with problems:

- Ignoring them and hoping that they will go away or that they will magically 'sort themselves out'

- Relying totally on someone else to come up with a solution

- Constantly worrying about what has caused the problem rather than thinking of possible solutions

- Relying on fate or luck to sort things out

- Becoming too distressed to deal with the problem

If you find that you're resorting to any of these 'methods', you might be putting yourself under unnecessary stress. A more effective way to deal with problems is to try to solve them yourself in a step-by-step way. Here's an example of how to solve a problem in a structured way.

Step 1: define the problem

First, try to work out what the actual problem is and be as specific as you can – this makes it easier to think of possible and appropriate solutions. For example, Anna has a problem with her daughter:

'I get anxious whenever I argue with my daughter about her excessive use of the telephone.'

Write down a problem you want to tackle in the space below:

_____

_____

_____

_____

Step 2: defining possible solutions

Once you've thought about the problem, write down as many solutions as you can think of in the table below – there are already examples for Anna's problem – and be as imaginative or outrageous as you like. Now look through your list of solutions and, like Anna has done, rate each solution from '–10' to '+10', where:

- '–10' indicates 'a very poor solution'

- '+10' indicates 'an extremely good solution'

- A rating of '0' indicates 'a solution with equal advantages and disadvantages'

Defining possible solutions

Anna's solutions	Rating
1 Leave the house whenever my daughter uses the telephone.	−9
2 Disconnect the telephone.	−5
3 Make her pay for her use of the telephone if it exceeds 'normal' usage.	+7
4 Consider what types of negative thoughts may be contributing to my anxiety about her using the telephone.	+8
5 Install a separate extension for her to use in her room.	+4

Defining possible solutions

Your solutions	Rating
1	
2	
3	
4	
5	
6	
7	
8	

Step 3: your best solution or combination of solutions

Now look through your list once again and decide which is the best solution to that particular problem. You might decide that there is more than one solution, or that a combination of solutions will work best. Anna decides to use a combination of these two solutions:

1 'Install another extension and make my daughter pay for her own telephone calls.'

2 'Examine my attitude about her use of the telephone and try to challenge any irrational thoughts that are causing unnecessary distress.'

Now write down a solution or solutions to your problem:

_____

_____

_____

_____

Step 4: how and when will you implement the solution?

Now think about how you will implement your solution to this problem. What is the best time to carry out your plan? Does the solution involve particular people or apply to certain places? Anna decides that this is how she'll implement her solution:

'I'll wait for the weekend when we're both at ease and then I'll talk to my daughter in her room about this problem and the solutions I think would be best.'

Now write down how you would implement your solution:

_____

_____

_____

_____

Step 5: review your efforts

Once you've tried a particular solution, it's important to review your efforts:

- How well did you manage to discuss this solution?

- Was it effective?

- If not, what can you do to improve it?

Put a cross on each of the scales below, to mark your solutions:

Easy to carry out	Neither easy nor difficult	Impossible
this solution	to carry out	to carry out

Outcome very	Outcome neither effective	Outcome very
effective	nor ineffective	ineffective

Learning how to solve your problems effectively can stop small problems growing into major sources of stress, which could make your panic symptoms worse. Try to identify the important problems that are playing on your mind and go through this exercise for each of them.

Summary

Review of Step 6

In Step 6 you've looked at how various combinations of techniques can work for you in different situations. For instance, to help control your anxiety you can use relaxation exercises before you go for a check-up at the dentist, and the breathing exercise while you're in the waiting room. And you can challenge and substitute negative thoughts, and practise the slow-breathing technique to help you deal with a visit to the supermarket. The most important thing is to identify the techniques that work best for you, and choose the right ones to use in different situations.

- Another useful way to prepare for a situation is to practise it in your mind – challenge the negative thoughts that come to mind and imagine the stressful situation while you use your coping strategies to control your anxiety. By doing this you can work through the imagined situation step-by-step and plan ahead to decide which anxiety-management strategies you'll use at each point. When you've successfully practised coping with a particular situation in your mind, you can try it out in 'real life'.

- Don't forget to reward yourself when you've had a success – however small a step you've taken. It's also important to track the progress you're making – from time to time, go back to your original list and re-rate each item as you manage to reduce the worry it causes you. As you start to overcome your anxiety, you'll see the 'anxiety ratings' drop for each of the situations on your list. A situation that you originally rated as '8' may now be a more manageable '3'.

- Don't take things too quickly – remember to work through your list of stressful situations steadily and systematically. Only move on to the more difficult situations when you're feeling more confident with the easier tasks and keep practising your coping skills regularly – it's easy to become disorganized or confused when you're anxious. Try to use the structured problem-solving technique to help overcome some of your sources of everyday stress.

Summary continues on next page

Summary

- Learning how to manage stress takes time and practice, so don't be discouraged if you still feel anxious even after you've been practising these skills for a while. Be patient and learn from your experiences – even the ones that don't turn out exactly the way you want them to. Try to remember that it's virtually impossible to remain anxious if you repeatedly expose yourself to a situation that's not really dangerous.

SECTION 4: Preventing Setbacks

This section will help you understand:

- Your pattern of recovery

- What relapse is

The six-step course you've just completed focuses on the techniques you can use to cope with stress and panic attacks. The more you practise, the easier it will become to use these techniques. But despite all your efforts, it might sometimes feel as if you're going backwards rather than forwards. It's easy to become demoralized by setbacks, especially when you've been making good progress. This last section looks at how you can prevent and overcome any setbacks.

Understanding your pattern of recovery

The 'normal' pattern of recovery from panic disorder and agoraphobia is often up and down – at times you may feel as if you've reached a plateau or that your anxiety is actually becoming worse again. The 'recovery graph' below shows how your recovery can be a bit of a bumpy ride.

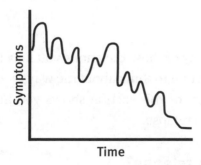

The normal pattern of recovery from panic disorder and agoraphobia

The graph shows that with time your symptoms tend to improve. But there may be days or even weeks when your symptoms flare up, just as there are times when your symptoms improve rapidly – perhaps even faster than you expected. In spite of these fluctuations, the important thing to remember is that if you keep on practising the techniques you've learnt, you'll gradually become less anxious and your symptoms will diminish or disappear completely.

What is relapse?

Relapse is when you experience a more serious setback – for instance when the panic symptoms you'd managed to overcome or control start to reappear. This can happen for a number of reasons, but as a first step it's important to work out whether you're having a 'relapse' or whether it's simply one of those 'downs' that are all part of the normal recovery process. Try answering the questions below if you become worried that you're having a relapse:

Checklist for relapse

1 Are you experiencing full-blown panic attacks?

Yes ☐   No ☐

2 Have your symptoms returned at the same intensity as when they first occurred?

Yes ☐   No ☐

3 Are the symptoms increasingly interfering with your usual daily routine?

Yes ☐   No ☐

4 Has the frequency of these symptoms increased to the same level as when you first started experiencing panic attacks?

Yes ☐   No ☐

If you've answered 'yes' to any of these questions you may be experiencing an early stage of relapse, so it's important to think about the ways you can prevent your symptoms getting worse. The rest of this section shows you how to stop any setbacks developing into a full-blown relapse.

Why might you have a relapse?

If you think you're experiencing a relapse it's usually down to a combination of things, such as everyday stresses getting on top of you again and not doing enough practice with the stress-management techniques you've learnt. And you may still find it difficult to 'label' what's a normal level of anxiety and what's not – even after you've recovered. So you might still mistake normal levels of stress – the feelings you get before an exam for instance – as the first signs of relapse. Ironically, simply worrying that you might be having a relapse may make it more likely that your panic symptoms will reappear.

Your chances of having a relapse also depend on how you deal with everyday stress. A number of things can influence the way you're affected by stress and whether this causes your panic symptoms to return. For instance, you may be particularly vulnerable to stress because you've been ill – or perhaps you've had an extremely busy couple of weeks at work, so you've been living on fast foods and missing out on enough sleep. Remember that the mind-body link means it's important to keep yourself physically healthy to stay in good shape psychologically.

Low self-esteem and a lack of confidence can also make you more vulnerable to anxiety symptoms. The same thing can happen if you give up practising your anxiety-reducing techniques too early, or you suddenly stop taking your prescribed anti-anxiety medicine or stop taking it too early. But if you feel that your symptoms have changed in character, or you can't put your finger on what's wrong, it's always best to talk to your doctor.

Preventing relapse

There are lots of things you can do to prevent relapse if you begin to feel stressed. If you answered 'yes' to any of the questions in the checklist for relapse (above) you may also find it useful to think about the following questions – these can help you pinpoint the best ways to stop a relapse. Circle 'Yes' or 'No' for each question.

1 Are there new stresses in your life?   Yes/No

Are you becoming overly sensitive to minor anxiety symptoms, which are making you worry unnecessarily?   Yes/No

If you've answered 'Yes' to either of these questions, it's a good idea to look again at Step 1 to refresh your memory about anxiety symptoms and the possible sources of stress. Try writing a list of the things that may have made your anxiety symptoms worse (you can use the Thoughts and Reflections pages at the end of this workbook). Are any of these stresses similar to the ones you listed back in Step 1, or are there new stresses that are adding to your worries?

2 Are you attempting to overcome your anxiety or avoidance of situations too quickly?   Yes/No

If you have a full-blown panic attack after weeks or months of having only minor anxiety symptoms, it's your body's way of warning you that you may be attempting to do too much too soon, or that you may not be doing enough preparation. Think about whether you've been pushing yourself too hard to overcome your avoidance of difficult situations. Or perhaps you need to do more preparation before you tackle these situations – such as muscle relaxation exercises or slow breathing.

It could be that you're becoming anxious about a new life challenge or change, such as a new job. Rather than simply worrying about what *might* happen, use the techniques you've learnt to assess the situation carefully before you plunge into it. You've now got the tools to help you cope with the tension you're feeling as a result of having to think about the change. But don't force yourself to take on the challenge unless it's essential. When you're thinking about taking on something new, the timing can be critical – if you do it too soon, or you don't prepare yourself properly, it can set back your recovery. If you do embark on a new venture, make sure that it doesn't interrupt the rest of your lifestyle and stress-management programme.

3 Are you still maintaining a healthy lifestyle?   Yes/No

It's easy to fall into bad habits and forget about the lifestyle factors that can affect your anxiety levels, especially if you haven't had any panic symptoms for a long time. It's a good idea to take a fresh look at your lifestyle from time to time, even if you're not experiencing any new feelings of anxiety. Check that you're eating a healthy diet, taking regular exercise and that you're not relying on stimulants like tea, coffee and cigarettes. And count up your weekly alcohol units – drinking too much can lower your threshold for panic.

It's also important to practise your relaxation exercises and slow-breathing techniques – make these part of your daily routine rather than something you use when you feel anxious. It takes time to master these techniques – if you don't keep practising them, your stress-management skills will become rusty.

4 Have you suddenly stopped taking your prescribed medicines, or have you been varying the dose?   Yes/No

If you stop taking your medicines or you suddenly change the dose, your anxiety symptoms can come back and you may start having panic attacks. Even if you feel that you've recovered, or you've seen a real improvement in your symptoms, it's important to talk to your doctor before you make any changes. If your doctor has changed your medication and you have a setback or relapse, book another appointment to discuss whether these symptoms are likely to pass quickly once you get used to the new treatment or whether you need to return to the original dose.

5. Are you lapsing into unhelpful ways of thinking?   Yes/No

If you're starting to have unhelpful thoughts, look back at the thinking exercises in Step 4 to challenge any negative interpretations of events, your feelings and your physical sensations and substitute them with more helpful, positive thoughts. It may help to go back to re-examining your thoughts in a systematic way – stop and ask yourself whether each thought is negative. Poor self-esteem and lack of confidence are directly related to negative thoughts, and vice versa. So by reinterpreting things in a more positive and helpful way, you can lift your self-esteem and confidence, which will make you less vulnerable to stress. Always remember to acknowledge your successes and reward yourself for coping with your anxiety symptoms.

If you work through these questions systematically, it will be easier to stop yourself slipping backwards. Keep your workbooks at hand so that you can go back to the exercises you learnt in Steps 1–6 to refresh your memory of how to overcome anxiety symptoms and panic attacks. If you feel that you're really not getting anywhere and you're still having panic attacks, talk to your doctor and perhaps ask for a referral to a mental health professional who specializes in the treatment of panic disorder. Remember that just because you have a setback, it doesn't mean that your anxiety symptoms will become as bad as they once were. By completing Steps 1–6, you've now got some very useful tools to deal with temporary setbacks, and you can usually put yourself back on the road to recovery very quickly.

Summary

- As you recover from panic disorder and agoraphobia there will be times when you feel that you're making little progress, or even going backwards. The 'normal' pattern of recovery is up and down, so try not to worry about this. The important thing is to keep on practising the techniques you've learnt – if you do this, you'll gradually become less anxious and you'll continue to recover.

- If you have a more serious setback – for instance if your anxiety symptoms start to reappear – you may be experiencing relapse. Try to work out whether this is what's happening, or whether you're just having a run of bad days. Work systematically through the 'preventing relapse' exercise in this section to pinpoint the best ways to stop any relapse.

- It can be useful to look back through your workbooks to refresh your memory on the techniques you've learnt. If this doesn't help, and your panic attacks have returned, talk to your doctor about getting some support from a mental health professional.

A Final Note

Now that you've worked through this self-help course, you're in a better position to take charge of your panic attacks and to participate fully again in all the activities you've been avoiding. Reread the books slowly if you find yourself slipping back to your old lifestyle or you start to think negatively – both of these things could increase the risk of your panic attacks recurring. And remember to practise the exercises regularly, even if you feel you've made a good recovery.

Overcoming panic and agoraphobia takes a lot of energy and commitment, so if you find that it's difficult to stay motivated you could think about joining a support group. It can be extremely helpful to hear how other people manage their symptoms and to share your experiences. To find out more about support groups, contact your doctor or local mental health service, or get in touch with some of the organizations listed at the back of this book. People with panic disorder and agoraphobia often find it particularly beneficial to attend a support group.

Finally, remember that even though your experience of anxiety may be painful, it's taught you valuable lessons about the impact of stress on your health and about the need to keep track of stress and deal with it as it occurs.

Useful Books

There are a number of other books that you may find useful in understanding panic disorder and agoraphobia. Some of these take a broad-based approach to dealing with stress in general. The more reading you do, the more likely it is that you'll pick up some useful skills for coping with panic attacks and agoraphobia. But remember to be selective and critical in deciding which techniques work best for you.

The following titles may be helpful.

Lee Baer, *Getting Control*, Little Brown, 1996.

Gillian Butler, *Overcoming Social Anxiety and Shyness*, Robinson, 1999.

Paul Foxman, *Dancing with Fear: Overcoming Anxiety in a World of Stress and Uncertainty*, Jason Aronson, 1999.

Paul Gilbert, *Overcoming Depression*, Robinson, 2000.

Mark Greener, *The Which? Guide to Managing Stress*, Which? Books, 1996.

Helen Kennerley, *Overcoming Anxiety*, Robinson, 1997.

Gerald L. Klerman *et al.* (eds), *Panic Anxiety and Its Treatments: Report of the World Psychiatric Association Presidential Educational Task Force*, New York, American Psychiatric Association, 1993.

Isaac Marks, *Living with Fear*, New York, McGraw-Hill, 1978.

Joy Melville, *Phobias and Obsessions*, Macdonald Optima, rev. ed. 1991.

Reneau Z. Peurifoy, *Anxiety, Phobias and Panic: Taking charge and conquering fear*, New York, Warner Books, 1995.

Stanley Rachman and Padmal de Silva, *Panic Disorders: The Facts*, Oxford University Publishing, 1996.

Shirley Swede and Seymour Jaffe, *The Panic Attack Recovery Book*, New York, New American Library-Dutton, 2000.

Robert E. Thayer, *The Origin of Everyday Moods: Managing energy, tension and stress*, Oxford University Publishing, 1996.

Shirley Trickett, *Coping with Anxiety and Depression*, Sheldon Press, 1989.

Useful Addresses

United Kingdom

Anxiety Disorders Association (formerly Phobic Action)
20 Church Street
Dagenham
Essex RM10 9RU
Tel: 020 8270 0999

British Association for Counselling and Psychotherapy
BACP House
35-37 Albert Street
Rugby
Warwickshire CV21 2SG
Tel: 0870 443 5252
Email: bacp@bacp.co.uk
Website: www.bacp.co.uk

First Steps to Freedom
24 Neville Road
Chichester
West Sussex PO19 3LX
Helpline: 0845 120 2916
Website: www.first-steps.org

Institute for Neuro-Physiological Psychology
INPP Ltd
1 Stanley Street
Chester CH1 2LR
Tel: 01244 311414
Email: support@inpp.org.uk

Lifeskills
Bowman House
6 Billetfield
Taunton
Somerset TA1 3NN
Tel: 01823 451771

MIND: The National Association for Mental Health
Granta House
15–19 Broadway
Stratford
London E15 4BQ
MindinfoLine: 0845 766 0163
(can also give you details of local tranquillizer withdrawal support groups)
Email: info@mind.org.uk

National Phobics Society (a self-help network)
Zion Community Resource Centre
339 Stretford Road
Hulme
Manchester M15 4ZY
Tel: 0870 122 2325
Email: info@phobics-society.org.uk
Website: www.phobics-society.org.uk

No Panic
93 Brands Farm Way
Randlay
Telford TF3 2JQ
Helpline: 01952 590545

Open Door Association
447 Pensby Road
Heswall
Wirral
Merseyside L61 9PQ
(No telephone number available)

Relaxation for Living (courses and information to combat stress)
Dunesk, 29 Burwood Park Road
Walton-on-Thames
Surrey KT12 5LH
Tel: 01932 227826

Triumph Over Phobia
(TOP UK)
PO Box 3760
Bath BA2 3WY
Tel: 0845 600 9601
Email: info@triumphoverphobia.org.uk
Website: www.triumphoverphobia.com

United States

American Mental Health Foundation
2 East 86th Street
New York
NY 1008
(Written enquiries only)

The Association for Behavioral and Cognitive Therapies
(formerly the Association for the Advancement of Behavior Therapy)
305 7th Avenue
New York
NY 10001
Tel: +1 212 647 1890
Website: www.aabt.org

The Behavior Therapy Center of New York
115 East 87th Street
New York
NY 10028
Tel: +1 212 410 6500

Behavioral Psychotherapy Center
23 Old Mamaroneck Road
White Plains
NY 10605
Tel: +1 914 761 4080

Institute for Behavior Therapy
137 East 36th Street
New York
NY 10016
Tel: +1 212 686 8778

Long Island Jewish Hospital at Hillside Phobia Clinic
New Hyde Park
NY 11040
Tel: +1 718 470 7000 (Hospital number)

Institutes for Neuro-Physiological Psychology
Dr Larry J. Beuret MD
4811 Emerson, Suite 209
Palatine
IL 60067
Tel: +1 847 303 1800

and

Mrs Victoria Hutton
6535 North Shore Way
Newmarket
Maryland 21774
Tel: +1 301 607 6752

White Plains Hospital Center
Anxiety and Phobia Clinic
Davis Ave., at Post Road
White Plains
NY 10601
Clinic tel: +1 914 681 0600
(Mon, Wed, Fri only, 9.00 a.m.– 4.00 p.m.)

Australia and New Zealand

Australian Capital Territory

Anxiety Support Group
Tel: +61 500 806 500

New South Wales

Mental Health Information Service
Tel: +61 2 9816 5688; 1800 674 200
Website: www.nswamh.org

Anxiety Disorders Foundation
Tel: +61 2 9963 3494
Fax: +61 2 9716 0416

Triumph Over Phobia
TOP NSW
PO BOX 213
Rockdale
New South Wales 2216
Australia

Northern Territory

Anxiety Disorders Foundation
Tel: +61 8 8927 9411

Queensland

Mental Health Association
Tel: +61 7 3358 4988
Fax: +61 7 3254 1027
Email: association@mentalhealth.org.au
Website: www.mentalhealth.org.au

Panic Anxiety Disorders Association
Tel: +61 7 3353 4851

Victoria

Anxiety Disorders Association
Tel: +61 3 9853 8089
Email: adavic@eisa.net.au
Website: home.vicnet.net.au/~adavic/

Anxiety Recovery Centre
PO Box 358 MT WAVERLEY VIC 3149
Tel: +61 3 9576 2477
Fax: +61 3 9576 2499
Email: arcmail@arcvic.com.au

Panic Anxiety Disorders Association
Tel: +61 3 9889 6760
Fax: +61 3 9889 1022
Email: tranx@alphalink.com.au
Website: www.tranx.org.au

Western Australia

Panic Anxiety Disorders Association
PO Box 130 NEDLANDS WA 6909
Tel: +61 8 9380 9898
Email: padawa@iinet.net.au

Extra Charts and Worksheets

Challenging negative thoughts

Situation	Negative thought	Challenging thought and considering an alternative

Challenging negative thoughts

Situation	Negative thought	Challenging thought and considering an alternative

Self-monitoring form for changing negative thoughts

Day/date	Negative thought	Anxiety level	Challenging thought	Positive/helpful thought

60

Self-monitoring form for changing negative thoughts

Day/date	Negative thought	Anxiety level	Challenging thought	Positive/helpful thought

Challenging and changing negative thoughts about physical sensations

Physical sensation	Negative thought	Challenging thought	Helpful thought

Challenging and changing negative thoughts about physical sensations

Physical sensation	Negative thought	Challenging thought	Helpful thought

Monitoring anxiety-provoking situations

Situation	Rating (0–10) 0 = no anxiety, 10 = highest level of anxiety	Change in rating		
		Week 1	Week 2	Week 3

Monitoring anxiety-provoking situations

Situation	Rating (0–10) 0 = no anxiety, 10 = highest level of anxiety	Change in rating		
		Week 1	Week 2	Week 3

Thoughts and Reflections

Thoughts and Reflections

Thoughts and Reflections

Thoughts and Reflections

Thoughts and Reflections

Thoughts and Reflections

Order further books in the Overcoming series

Quantity	Title	Price	Total
	An Introduction to Coping with Anxiety (pack of 10 booklets)	£10.00	
	An Introduction to Coping with Depression (pack of 10 booklets)	£10.00	
	An Introduction to Coping with Health Anxiety (pack of 10 booklets)	£10.00	
	An Introduction to Coping with Panic (pack of 10 booklets)	£10.00	
	An Introduction to Coping with Phobias (pack of 10 booklets)	£10.00	
	An Introduction to Coping with Obsessive Compulsive Disorder (pack of 10 booklets)	£10.00	
	Overcoming Anxiety Self-Help Course	£21.00	
	Overcoming Bulimia Nervosa and Binge-Eating Self-Help Course	£21.00	
	Overcoming Low Self-Esteem Self-Help Course	£21.00	
	Overcoming Panic and Agoraphobia Self-Help Course	£21.00	
	Overcoming Social Anxiety and Shyness Self-Help Course	£21.00	
	Overcoming Anger and Irritability	£9.99	
	Overcoming Anorexia Nervosa	£9.99	
	Overcoming Anxiety	£9.99	
	Bulimia Nervosa and Binge-Eating	£9.99	
	Overcoming Childhood Trauma	£9.99	
	Overcoming Chronic Fatigue	£9.99	
	Overcoming Chronic Pain	£9.99	
	Overcoming Compulsive Gambling	£9.99	
	Overcoming Depression	£9.99	
	Overcoming Insomnia and Sleeping Problems	£9.99	
	Overcoming Low Self-Esteem	£9.99	
	Overcoming Mood Swings	£9.99	
	Overcoming Obsessive Compulsive Disorders	£9.99	
	Overcoming Panic	£9.99	
	Overcoming Paranoid and Suspicious Thoughts	£9.99	
	Overcoming Problem Drinking	£9.99	
	Overcoming Relationship Problems	£9.99	
	Overcoming Sexual Problems	£9.99	
	Overcoming Social Anxiety and Shyness	£9.99	
	Overcoming Traumatic Stress	£9.99	
	Overcoming Weight Problems	£9.99	
	Overcoming Your Smoking Habit	£9.99	
	P & P	FREE	
		Grand TOTAL £	

Name:

Delivery address:

Postcode:

Daytime tel. no.:

Email:

How to pay:

1. **By telephone**: call the TBS order line on 01206 522 800 and quote OPDSHC. Phone lines are open between Monday – Friday, 8.30am – 5.30pm.

2. **By post**: send a cheque for the full amount payable to TBS Ltd. and send form to:

   Freepost RLUL-SJGC-SGKJ,
   Cash Sales/Direct Mail Dept.,
   The Book Service,
   Colchester Road, Frating,
   Colchester CO7 7DW